Rick's Gum
and
The Red Pot

Level 2 – Red

Helpful Hints for Reading at Home

The graphemes (written letters) and phonemes (units of sound) used throughout this series are aligned with Letters and Sounds. This offers a consistent approach to learning whether reading at home or in the classroom.

HERE IS A LIST OF PHONEMES FOR THIS PHASE OF LEARNING. AN EXAMPLE OF THE PRONUNCIATION CAN BE FOUND IN BRACKETS.

Phase 2			
s (sat)	a (cat)	t (tap)	p (tap)
i (pin)	n (net)	m (man)	d (dog)
g (go)	o (sock)	c (cat)	k (kin)
ck (sack)	e (elf)	u (up)	r (rabbit)
h (hut)	b (ball)	f (fish)	ff (off)
l (lip)	ll (ball)	ss (hiss)	

HERE ARE SOME WORDS WHICH YOUR CHILD MAY FIND TRICKY.

Phase 2 Tricky Words			
the	to	I	no
go	into		

TOP TIPS FOR HELPING YOUR CHILD TO READ:

• Allow children time to break down unfamiliar words into units of sound and then encourage children to string these sounds together to create the word.

• Encourage your child to point out any focus phonics when they are used.

• Read through the book more than once to grow confidence.

• Ask simple questions about the text to assess understanding.

• Encourage children to use illustrations as prompts.

This book focuses on the phonemes /u/ and /r/ and is a red level 2 book band.

Rick's Gum and The Red Pot

Written by
William Anthony

Illustrated by
Drue Rintoul

Can you say this sound and draw it with your finger?

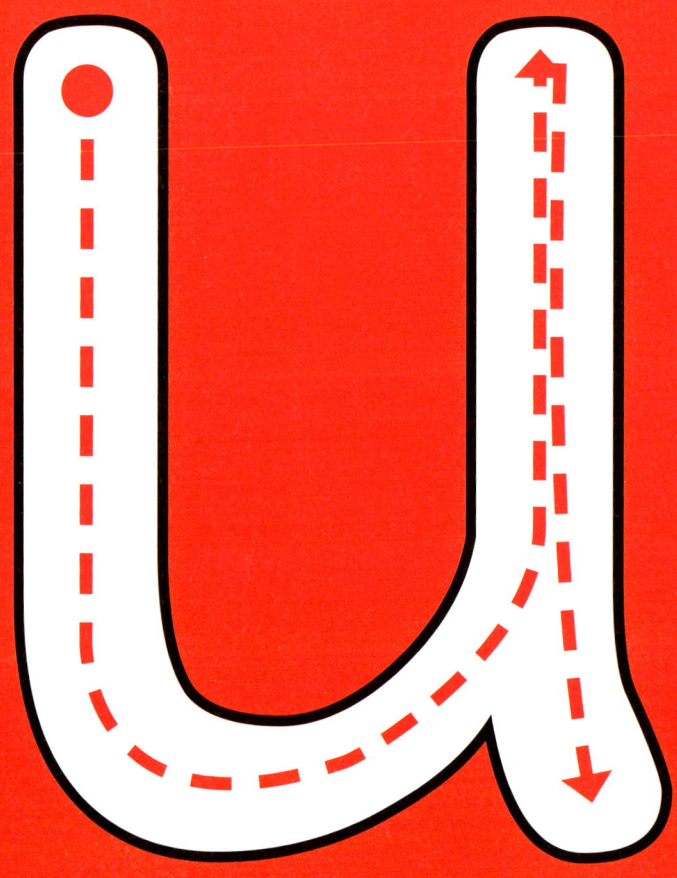

Rick's Gum

Written by
William Anthony

Illustrated by
Drue Rintoul

Rick got the gum. It is in.

The red gum did not pop.

Rick can run. Rick can go.

"Run, Mum."
Mum is on the rug.

"Run, Nan."
Nan is in the mud.

"Run, Dad."
Dad is in the pit.

Rick can go up. Up up up.

Can Rick go up to the Sun?

It can pop the gum. Go Rick go.

The gum is a dud. Mum and Nan get Rick.

Dad is in the pit.

Rick gets Dad the gum. Dad is up.

Can you say this sound and draw it with your finger?

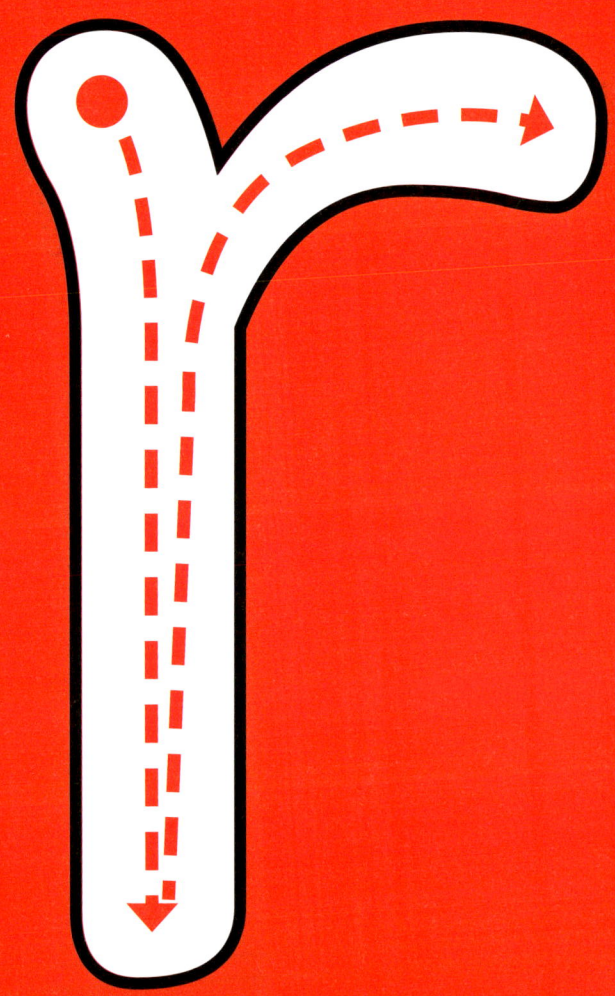

The Red Pot

Written by
William Anthony

Illustrated by
Drue Rintoul

Can Rem get a tick on the sum? No.

Rem is mad. Rem gets the red pot.

Rem can get red on the rim.

Rem can get red on the sum.

Rem can get red on the rug.

Rem can get red on the pup.

Rem can get red on the rib.

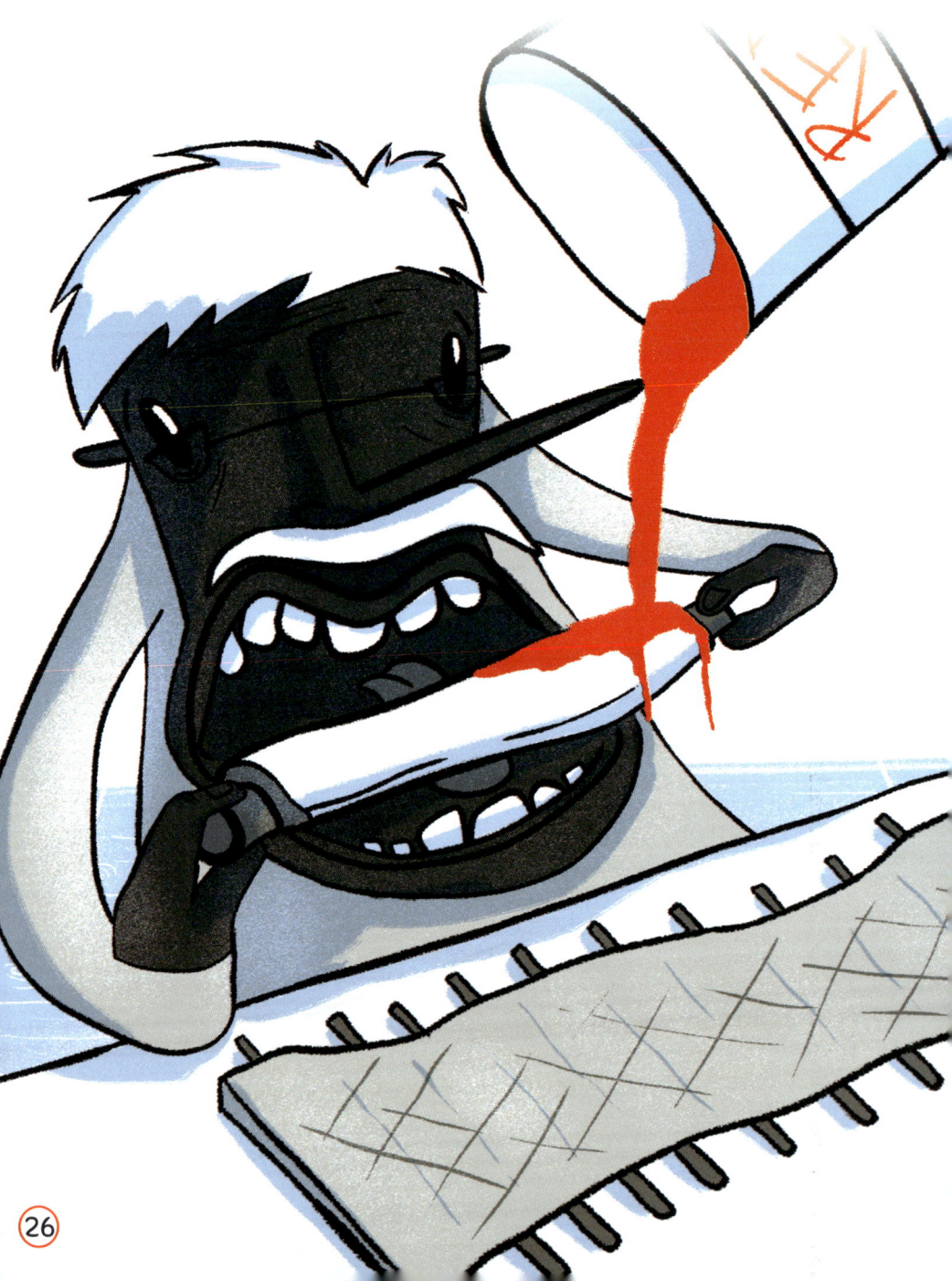

Rem can get red in the mug.

Rem can get red on Mum.

Rem can get red on Dad.

No, Rem. No. Not on us.

Rem can get red on us!

©2022 **BookLife Publishing Ltd.**
King's Lynn, Norfolk, PE30 4LS, UK

ISBN 978-1-80155-803-7

All rights reserved. Printed in Poland.
A catalogue record for this book is available from the British Library.

Rick's Gum and The Red Pot
Written by William Anthony
Illustrated by Drue Rintoul

An Introduction to BookLife Readers...

Our Readers have been specifically created in line with the London Institute of Education's approach to book banding and are phonetically decodable and ordered to support each phase of Letters and Sounds.

Each book has been created to provide the best possible reading and learning experience. Our aim is to share our love of books with children, providing both emerging readers and prolific page-turners with beautiful books that are guaranteed to provoke interest and learning, regardless of ability.

BOOK BAND GRADED using the Institute of Education's approach to levelling.

PHONETICALLY DECODABLE supporting each phase of Letters and Sounds.

EXERCISES AND QUESTIONS to offer reinforcement and to ascertain comprehension.

BEAUTIFULLY ILLUSTRATED to inspire and provoke engagement, providing a variety of styles for the reader to enjoy whilst reading through the series.

AUTHOR INSIGHT:
WILLIAM ANTHONY

William Anthony's involvement with children's education is quite extensive. He has written and edited many titles for BookLife Publishing across a wide range of subjects. William graduated from Cardiff University with a 1st Class BA (Hons) in Journalism, Media and Culture, creating an app and a TV series, among other things, during his time there.

William Anthony has also produced work for the Prince's Trust, a charity created by HRH The Prince of Wales, that helps young people with their professional future. He has created animated videos for a children's education company that works closely with the charity.

This book focuses on the phonemes /u/ and /r/ and is a red level 2 book band.